A-B-C
Mazes

Viki Woodworth

Dover Publications, Inc.
Mineola, New York

Note

There are 48 mazes in this little book—and each one has important words that begin with a letter of the alphabet. Look carefully, and you will find that the mazes are in A-B-C order: the puzzles start off with an **artist**, a **bear**, and a **clown**! All except for ox, which **ends** with **x**. It's hard to find words that begin with **x**!

Each maze shows a path leading from **start** to **end.** Get your pencil ready and help a **canary** reach its **cage** (keeping away from a **cat**!), show a **king** the path to take to reach his **keys**, find the way for a **rooster** to get to a **rooftop**, and there are many more challenges. Try to finish all of the mazes before checking the Solutions, which begin on page 52. You can have even more fun by coloring in all of the puzzle pages with colored pencils or crayons. Let's get started!

This **artist** needs the **a**pples to make his painting.
Show him the way to get to them.

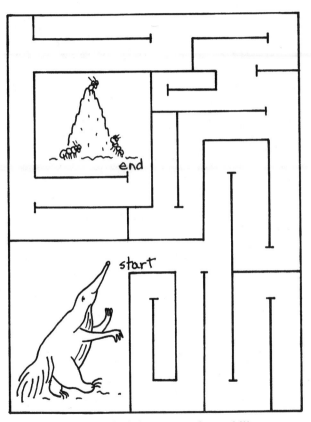

Help the **a**nteater find the way to the **a**nthill.

The bear is looking for the berries. Help it find the way to this tasty treat.

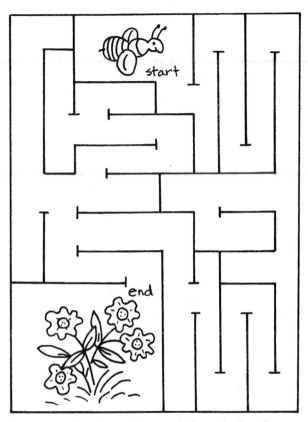

start

end

Do you see the pretty **b**lossoms? Show the **b**ee the way to reach them.

start

end

Hurry! Help the clown find the way to get to this car!

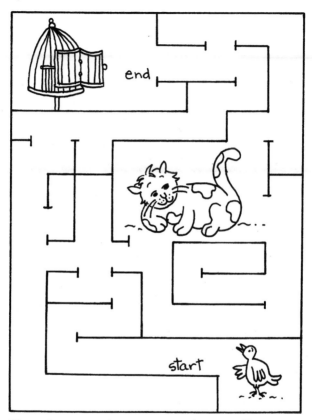

end

start

Show the **c**anary how to get to the **c**age. Keep away
from the **c**at!

start

end

Can you help this **d**og get to the **d**oghouse? He'll be so happy!

10

The **d**uck would like to visit its friend, the **d**ragonfly. Please show it the way.

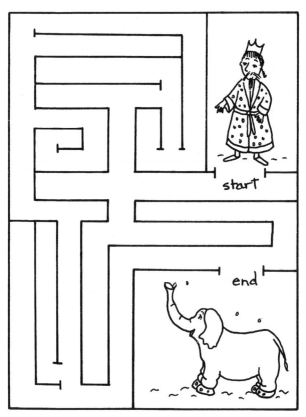

start

end

The emperor has lost his elephant! Show him the way to find it.

12

This young **elf** is lost. Please help him find the way to **Elf** Land.

start

end

The **f**ox is in the henhouse again. Help the **f**armer get there quickly!

Help the **fl**y get away from the **f**rog. Show it the way to
the end of the path.

The **g**oat is trying to find the way to the **g**ate. Please help it get there.

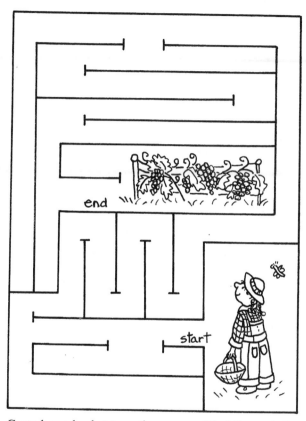

Greta has a basket to **g**ather **g**rapes. Find the path for her to take.

This **h**en wants to get **h**ome to her **h**ouse back at the farm. Help her find the way.

18

The **h**ummingbird smells the sweet **h**oneysuckle flowers.
Show it the way to get to them.

There are some lovely irises at the end of the path.
Help the insect find the way to reach them.

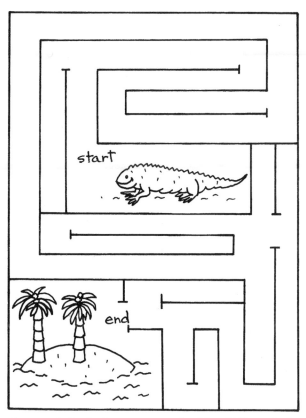

start

end

Can you help the **i**guana get to the **i**sland? Show it the best way to get there.

The **jaguar** needs to get to its home in the **jungle**. Can you show it the way?

22

start

end

Jackrabbit's **jump** rope is at the end of the path.
Please help **J**ackrabbit find the way there.

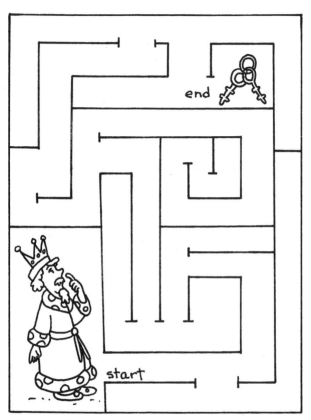

Oh, no! The **k**ing has lost his **k**eys! Help him find them at the end of the path.

The **k**angaroo is playing hide-and-seek with the **k**itten. Show the **k**angaroo the way to the end of the path, where the **k**itten is hiding.

25

The llama can't wait to get to those leaves at the end of the trail. Won't you help it find the way there?

start

end

A pot of lollipops waits at the end of the path. Help the leprechaun get to this treat.

start

end

Won't you show this hungry **m**onkey the way to the pile of **m**angoes?

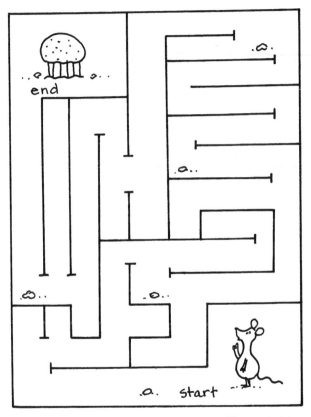

end

start

The **m**ouse wants to get to the sweet **m**uffin. Help him get there. He can eat five **m**uffin bits along the way.

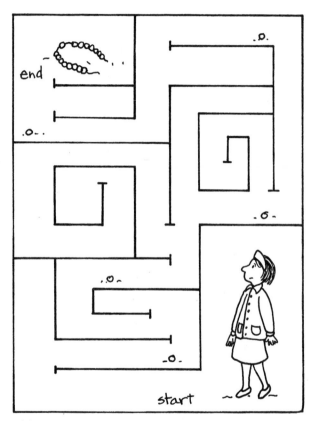

end

start

This nurse broke her necklace. You can help her by taking the right path to pick up five beads.

It's time for the nightingale to return to its nest. Please show it the way to get there.

The **o**strich and the **o**wl have a playdate. Help the **o**strich get to the end of the path, where the **o**wl is waiting.

32

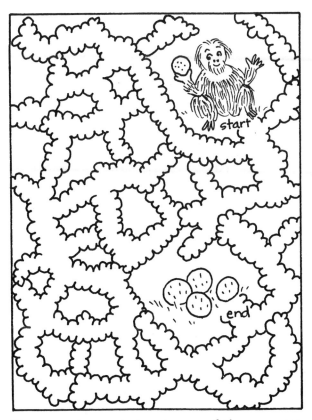

The **o**rangutan wants to eat some of those **o**ranges. Show it the way to get to the **o**ranges.

Help the **p**arrot find its way back to the **p**irate. Show
it the path to take to get there.

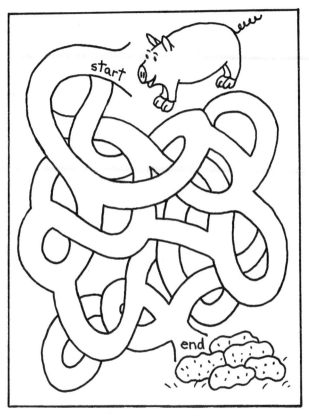

The **p**ig knows that a bunch of crunchy **p**otatoes is at the end of the path. Please help the **p**ig get to them.

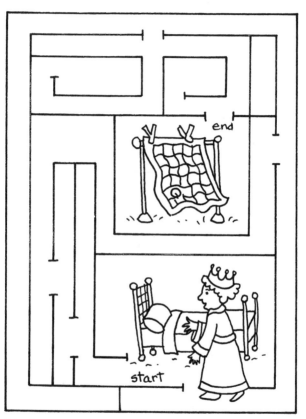

It's time to make the bed! Help the **q**ueen get to her
quilt at the end of the path.

The sun's coming up, and the **r**ooster needs to crow!
Show the **r**ooster the way to get to the **r**ooftop.

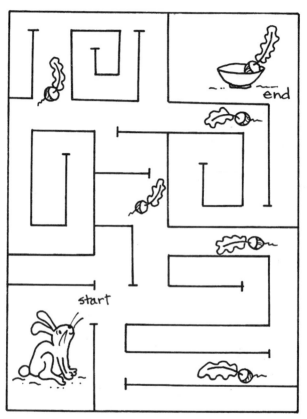

The rabbit needs to pick up five radishes to put in the bowl at the end of the trail. Please show it the way to go.

Hurry! The sailor has to get to this ship before it leaves! Show him how to get to it.

A bunch of yummy strawberries is growing at the end of the path. Please help the snail get to them.

The toad knows that a big treasure chest is nearby. Help the toad find the best way to get to it.

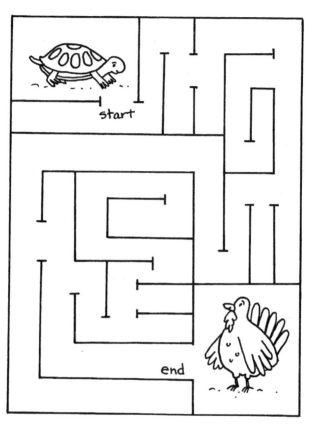

start

end

The turkey is waiting for the turtle so that they can go for a walk. Show the turtle how to get to the turkey.

42

start

end

Even a **u**nicorn needs an **u**mbrella in the rain. Help this **u**nicorn find its way to the **u**mbrella.

The **u**mpire can't do his job without his **u**niform.
Please show him the way to get to it.

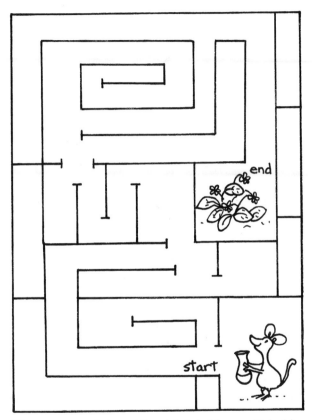

end

start

The mouse wants to put the violets in his vase. Take him
along the path to reach the bunch of violets at the end.

This vulture has a valentine card for his friend. Won't you show him the way to go to get to her?

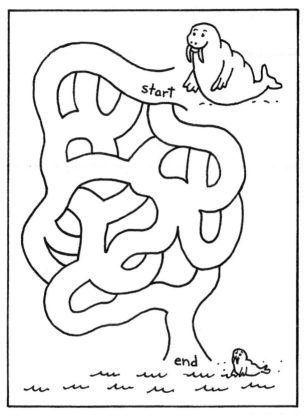

start

end

The walrus wants to dive into the waves. Help it find
its way back to the water.

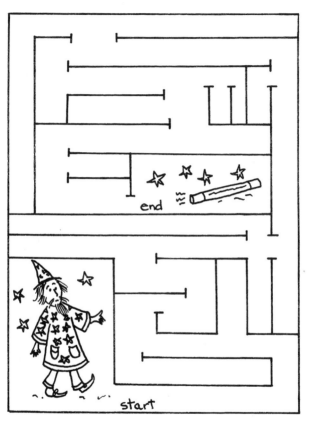

Help this wizard get to his wand. He needs it right away to cast a spell!

end

start

This ox is learning to play the xylophone. Show it the path to take to get to it.

start

end

The **yo-yo** has rolled away from the **yak**. Please help the yak find its way to the **yo-yo**.

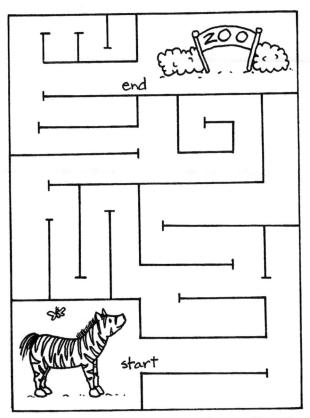

It's time for the zebra to return to the zoo. Show the zebra the best way to get back.

Solutions

page 4

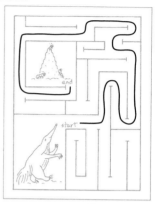

page 5

page 6

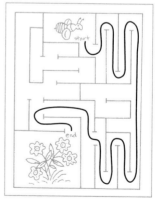

page 7

page 8

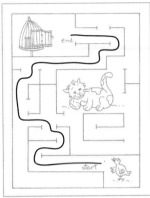

page 9

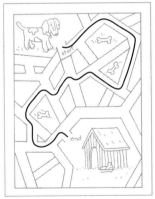

page 10

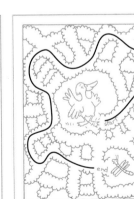

page 11

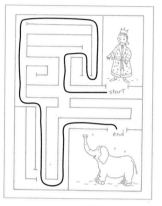

page 12

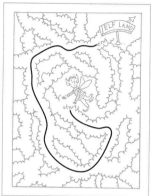

page 13

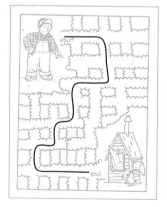

page 14

page 15

54

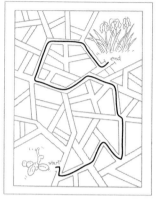

page 20

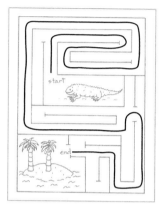

page 21

page 22

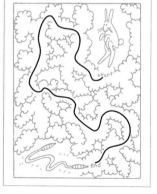

page 23

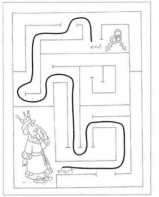

page 24

page 25

page 26

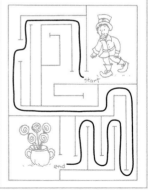

page 27

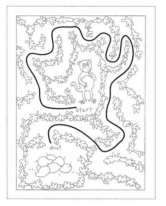

page 28

page 29

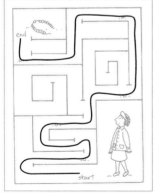

page 30

page 31

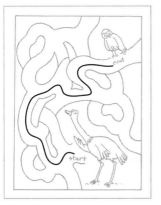

page 32

page 33

page 34

page 35

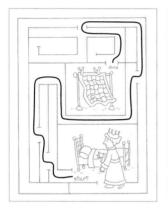

page 36

page 37

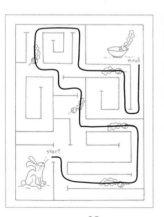

page 38

page 39

page 40

page 41

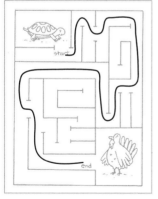

page 42

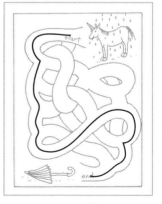

page 43

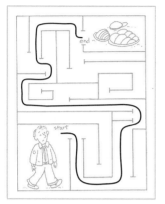

page 44

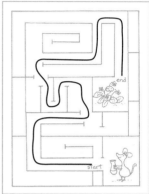

page 45

page 46

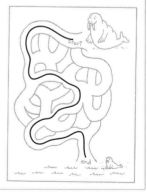

page 47

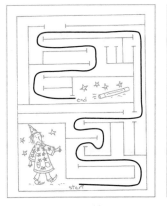

page 48

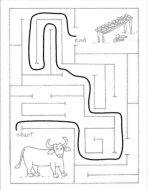

page 49

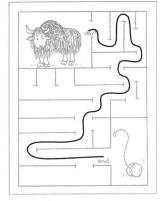

page 50

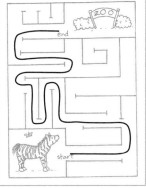

page 51

63